Confessions of a Stutterer

poems by

Tyson Higel

Finishing Line Press
Georgetown, Kentucky

Confessions
of a
Stutterer

ACKNOWLEDGMENTS

My gratitude to the editors of the publications in which the following poems
appeared:

redrosethorns: "The More the Merrier" & "The Hardened Ground of Shame"
York Literary Review: "Oy Vey"

Publisher: Leah Huete de Maines
Editor: Christen Kincaid
Cover Art: Nicolò Canova
Author Photo: Bodi Hallett (Sattva Photo)
Cover Design: Elizabeth Maines McCleavy

Order online: www.finishinglinepress.com
also available on amazon.com

Author inquiries and mail orders:
Finishing Line Press
PO Box 1626
Georgetown, Kentucky 40324
USA

Contents

The Shelter I Build 1

Deception 2

Again and Again and Again and Again 3

Confessions of a Stutterer 4

(Sweeping) Insecurities 7

Impediments of My Oration 8

Flip 9

The Black and White of It 10

Days of Oscillation 11

Little Blue Towel 12

This Minus That 13

The False Finish Line 14

Juggling 15

I'm Listening 16

Being Seen at the Hospital 17

Injection Conjecture 18

Into the Background 19

Oy Vey 20

A Love Story with Hope 21

I Sometimes Stutter; I Plead Your Grace 22

The Put-Together Pedestal 23

Forgiving Grace 24

Baring the Unbearable 25

The More the Merrier 27

The Hardened Ground of Shame 28

The Shelter I Build

People are often surprised
when I tell them that I stutter,
or when they hear it for the first time.
I've become good at hiding it,
sheltering it from day's light.
Much too bright for the shadow it casts.

But its hiding never lasts.
Even if I can pass as fluent,
substituting words, recasting what I say,
there are still moments of stark contrast—
a block, prolongation, s-s-stutter—that blasts
my shadow's shelter, at long last, apart.

It inevitably happens, but not always quick.
The shelter's made of brick; well-concealing
for the thick shadow of speech that is my secret.
I reconstruct it every time I talk, carefully pick
the words that'll click together fluently.
A halting cadence that tricks some, but not me.

I may pass as fluent, but I'm hardly free
to give you my two cents; more like a penny,
for only half of what I mean to say
is what I'm able to speak.
Half-expressions, half of my being
never fully seen,

 hidden in the shelter I build.

Deception

It was another day of getting by,
passing,
trying to avoid misinterpretation.
Life's and my creation,
this hiding;
deception in the name of dignity.
And even that I don't have fully.

Again and Again and Again and Again

I had a decent day of speaking, up until,
leaving the hospital, I stopped to chitchat
with a colleague.

I write to process feelings like this,
of embarrassment;
because what transpired
was certainly embarrassing:

my fluency fell flat—
unable to rise to
convivial conversation
about how their day had been,
and other niceties.

It's these moments of awkwardness,
awkward for me
and them,
that I wish I could replay,
and retry,
again

and again,

and again
and again.

Confessions of a Stutterer

This poem is confessional
and contextual-adding
for those who don't already know.

I write because I'm most clear on the page;
because, often, I'm unclear in what I say
when speaking verbally.

My speech is impeding, and that's ok.
There's much worse one can be assailed by
in the human condition.

But I'm aware that,
in my interactions with you,
it impairs my ability to be true
to my intentions.

I don't intend to be smug.
I don't intend to be halting.
I don't intend to be confusing,
or indirect.

And I don't intend to infect conversations
with unease, or intensity.

Let me address these concerns,
whether untrue,
or if you, too,
have recognized those that I mentioned,
which sever mutual connection.

Where do I begin?

Let's try a metaphor:
verbal expression is like a door—
often times unlocked,
allowing easy accessibility.

In these moments,
I can walk my words to you
with the cadence I always wish for.

But sometimes, the door is locked.
And in those moments,
the clock ticks while I attempt to talk
in the way that I intend.

It's hesitance, while I pick the lock
of the door that's blocking
what I'd like to convey,
and how I'd like to phrase it for you.

After moments that may have
already distracted your focus,
or confused you,
I then, finally, come through the door
with the words that I'd pined for.

And in that struggle, you might see,
across the door's window
separating you and me,
involuntary movements on my face.

I wish it weren't the case.
Quivers in my eyebrows, and lips,
are like slivers
in non-verbal communication
that lead to misinterpretation.

And other times, while trying to
unlock the door of speech,
I simply can't,
and resort to trudging around it
until I finally reach you.

But when I do,
much has been lost in translation.
Because that's what happens—
I'm forced to translate the words
I want to say
to ones I won't filet.

It's not just the words, either.
It, too, is how I intonate them for you.
A fluctuation in tone
can hang heavily in the room;
to a point, unsettling.

With all that said,
from my head to yours,
I apologize for
how I've made you feel,
I'm sure,
on the other side of that door.

(Sweeping) Insecurities

Sweeping away the leaves
blown constantly onto the sidewalk
by an unforgiving wind.
It howls inside my head,
scattering them day and night
into unkept piles of damp foliage
stuck to the cement of my mind.

       I'm sweeping.

          I'm sweeping.

Impediments of My Oration

My speech, I can feel,
is about to fail me.
And with that I'm faced
with two ways to proceed:

I can circumlocute,
use words I'm forced to choose;
avoid disfluent remorse
at the risk of sounding a fool.

Or I can use the words I wish
and endure the stuttering moments
through the brook of suffering,
sure to make me look foolish.

Wading in my conversations,
ripe with misinterpretation.
So often do I land amiss
—impediments of my oration.

Flip

Clouds curl over the sky
as I
lie in the grass and watch.

Moving ever so slightly slow
they blow,
towing the forecast with.

But here I remain, in place,
in case
grace lets light pierce through.

All I'm asking for is a glimpse,
and hence,
absence of joy will flip.

The Black and White of It

I can hardly speak
but sing hardily,
      for reasons that I do not know.
I'm fluent in song,
but when I talk, it's all wrong—
      the words and the rhythm of flow.
I stammer and stutter
but musically flutter
      along a dull peak like a crow.
I'm either black like the bird,
      or white, like the snow.

Days of Oscillation

Oscillating,
never the same person
day to day.

My moods change;
my bandwidth frays:
white and grey and black.

In the spectrum, there's shame—
an inability to remain at one's best,
day to day.

Is it my fault, this drain?
Is it society's expectations?
What's to blame for how I feel?

Day to day.

Little Blue Towel

Lying on the street
was a little blue towel.
As cars drove by,
it fluttered
and whirled,
blown to new positions
and configurations,
folded,
never ideally flat.

I empathize with that towel.

This Minus That

Trying to find a formula to always be one's best self
is exhausting,
seeming as though nothing solves the issue you've been dealt.
You try this, try that, try something else,
tossing every possible solution into contention.
And tossed, too, is a prayer for equilibrium,
to find suspension in what supports us, and allows
the best version of ourselves to enact
from then on, now.

The False Finish Line

"If I could only speak freely . . .
life would be more
bearable;
livable;
enjoyable."

—The false finish line
I so faithfully stumble toward.

Juggling

Juggling constantly,
so it seems:

      Expression

                    Connection

      Reflection

Where, to me,
has Connection flung?

I'm Listening

Little bird in a big tree.
Who are you calling out to?
To me?
You're alone and so am I.
Is what you say a cry?
Or do I misconstrue?
Whatever it is, I'm listening.

Being Seen at the Hospital

I was assigned to a patient today
who'd had a stroke in the past,
and who now had expressive aphasia.

She struggled with speaking,
delayed by her brain that kept seeking and seeking
the words that she wished to compel from her mouth.

And if the words *were* found by her mind,
she would try to say them, but was often blocked
by an invisible bind that stopped her communication.

I could see the frustration she felt while we spoke.
It's a feeling I encounter every day, and disclosed
that I stutter and know, in a way, the experience.

There's a dreariness that takes over you
when you're unable to speak your mind.
Will you be listened to in kind, and, at all, taken serious?

There's enough of us who know this much too well,
unfortunately;
who know that assumptions are impediments all their own.

It's why I told her speaking for me, too, is difficult.
I wanted her to feel comfortable,
that she was seen and understood.

And what I received, from the goodness of her heart,
was a smile that showed that she,
also, saw me.

Injection Conjecture

"Any questions?"
asked the nurse,
after giving the shot.

I thought.

"What's the meaning of life?"

Answered not, he,
and directed the question
back at me.

I thought.

"To express
and to be felt
and to feel."

Into the Background

In a room of personalities
predominate with humor,
and quick wit,
I find myself receding
away from them, and it—
the jokes, remarks, and quips;
the faster-than-I-can-keep-up-with banter.
I'm contemplative by nature,
and if I can't,
or think I can't,
add to the dialogue,
I'll write it on the page
whereon I sing my songs.

Oy Vey

Fumbling through life
in a world of verbal communication.
I try to speak, but am only able
to mumble and gurgle partial phrases:
half-truths of my expression,
never fully articulated.
And there lies my consternation.
It's the difficulty in participating,
trying to exchange pieces of my mind,
of my being;
my thoughts on the way I see things.
They get tied up within me,
unspoken for.
"So quiet."
"No personality."
"What a bore."
Are these righteous fears
of what others see and think of me?
Or are they only fictitious, to be ignored?
My vocal cords are never direct
to the truth of what I want to say,
so is it far-fetched thinking
that my mind might, too, be indirect
to the truth of others' perceptions?
Oy vey.

A Love Story with Hope

The frustrating thing about existing,
is the hope that springs from revelation
doesn't last.

You think you'll be changed from that instant on.
That you'll finally move past the old ways.
That a switch has been flipped.

But change doesn't happen that quick.
You unlearn and relearn.
Apply, and try, and feel ungratified

until a pattern emerges
from all the self-work that you've done,
and some memory of that initial frustration

flirts with your sense of hope again.

I Sometimes Stutter; I Plead Your Grace

I haven't forgotten my name,
no; it's my speech that comes out lame.
My vocal cords, they aren't so tame.
They're often not in my control.
Unreal it seems; you crack a joke.
Smiled or not, I soon after spoke:

        I sometimes stutter; I plead your grace.

My mission isn't to inflame
within you any sense of shame.
My only wish is to reclaim
what stuttering, alone, has stole:
my dignity—it's nearly broke,
but helps to openly uncloak:

        I sometimes stutter; I plead your grace.

In doing so, it lessens shame;
knows, the listener, what's to blame,
which then creates a whole new frame
for empathizing with the soul.
You're now aware—on words, I choke.
And with more others, I'll invoke:

        I sometimes stutter; I plead your grace.

The Put-Together Pedestal

Why is it that we often
put people we're meeting for the first time
on a pedestal?
Thinking they've no issues or insecurities
that are affecting their meeting of us
like it is for ourselves,
within.

The idea's bullshit—
that everyone is put together,
no loose ends that

get

away from us,

in all our moments.

Forgiving Grace

Let it dissolve,
disintegrate.
The solution lies in assimilating the event.

What happened
did happen.

Let's say it again:
What happened *did* happen,
but your fate is not tied to what occurred.
You are more than the event;
you're resilient,
I assure you.

It's not to be adjourned with,
but to learn from and maybe,
even, forgive
whomever it is that needs it,

including ourselves.

Baring the Unbearable

It's hard to be vulnerable.
It's embarrassing to be vulnerable.
I know it every time I stutter,
and break eye contact.

Suspended, without grasp,
on the cadence of my words
—time passing.

Is your attention passing?
Is your interest waning?
The levee isn't breaking,
and the force of my throat tightening
hardly produces a crack.

It's uncomfortable to be vulnerable,
and taxing on my mind if
my vulnerability's made you so.
I want you to know that.

I want every person I've spoken to
—the barista who takes my order;
the stranger who chats with me
in line at the grocery store;
the friend who listens to me
think aloud these thoughts I wrote—
I want them all to know
that I grieve every time
the greatest of my insecurities
makes a show of itself.

And while being vulnerable is
hard,
and embarrassing,
and uncomfortable,
it has bore my unguarded self
to all those I've spoken to.

And in baring the unbearable,
more of me is known.
Isn't that, ultimately,
what we wish for?

The More the Merrier

Bright Christmas lights
shine on the front of a house,
above the porch and front door
and windows facing north;
but not on the house's sides,
where it's dark and unseen in full,
where it's not been made a scene, at all.

And we, like houses,
don't want to make a scene of ourselves,
don't want to be seen for all we are;
don't want attention to our uglier walls,
undecorated and scarred, and broken;
don't want to be seen wide open,
to all the imperfections we hide.

And so we only shine lights on our facade,
the presentable sides of ourselves;
not the odd walls that hide in the shadows.
And maybe that makes us shallow,
and not three-dimensional;
not seen in full, and for what we can fully be.

Let all of your lights shine.

Go through life in all your beauty.

The Hardened Ground of Shame

To be utterly honest
is to radicalize your truth.

It is a reformation.
It is a reclamation.
It is for *you*.

But it's for others, too—
mutuality acknowledged, and known,
and in the knowing,
a new relationship may be sown.

For then,
and only then,
is the scope understood.
Clues may have come prior,
(subtle; overt)
but to be spoken of openly
is the only way it would.

On your terms,
and their agreement,
acceptance can be reached.
Through courage, and love,
the hardened ground of shame can be breached
by our effort to see
the light of life above.

Born and raised in Nebraska, **Tyson Higel** now lives on the Washington state coast where he works as a nurse. He began writing poetry in search of fluent self-expression, something he struggles with as a person who stutters. It's on the page that he's found his voice, and it's his hope to not only be read, but, ultimately, to be heard. His poetry has appeared in *York Literary Review,* *redrosethorns, The Broadkill Review, Rabble Review, and Corridor,* among others. For more, visit tysonhigel.mailchimpsites.com